Sidewalk
Prayers

To
Jude, Jean, and Dexter
for having enriched our family
with their faith and love

Sidewalk Prayers

Orlando L. Tibbetts

JUDSON PRESS, Valley Forge

SIDEWALK PRAYERS

International Standard Book No. 0-8170-0489-0
Library of Congress Catalog Card No. 71-139501

Printed in the U.S.A.

Contents

Introduction

It was in the home of the Rev. David Sheppard, at the May-flower Family Centre in Canning Town, London, that I decided to write this book. Members of his congregation, who are laboring people amongst the docks of East Side, London, were discussing, "How can we make our church more effective?" Several of these were young people who suggested that the church was not speaking their language. They urged radical changes in the worship service with the elimination of "Thees," "Thous," "hasts," and "wasts." For some time I had been uncomfortable about the devotional life of my family and my church; we were speaking the language of another era and these young people were speaking for the young church of the world! That's when I decided to change my praying ways. I had used my last "Thou" in prayer.

This led me to examine carefully my own prayer life—both public and private. Why did I use certain words and certain forms? Because I had been taught that you address God in only one way, as King, Authority, the far-removed Creator, or even the almost unmentionable. This, however, is really a cultural carry-over from a day which no longer communicates to the needs of common man. I was reminded of the fact that when Jesus prayed the Lord's Prayer and used the term, "Our Father," he was addressing God in a rather shocking and radical way for the world in which he lived; but he was also using a form which had meaning for common men and that's why they followed him!

The reason so many have stopped praying is their reluctance to mouth the vocabulary of King James and to express themselves to their God and Father in terms which make

7

them feel uncomfortable and artificial. Thus the following prayers are my own outpourings without thought of cultural acceptance. They are the result of many years of shepherding people in the local parish as well as relating to them as fellow laborers in a foreign country and as urban workers amongst the crises of our times.

The other writings came at times of travel, walking through the city streets, while in urban crises meetings, riding on the subway, or participating in worship services. I make no claim to divine inspiration; yet I could not contain myself from writing what I felt.

The Scripture portions called "Sidewalk Bible Headlines" are not intended to be authentic, authorized Bible translations. They are an attempt to put those verses into language which has meaning for today. They combine urban imagery with ordinary language.

In other words, my hope in writing this book is to start something within the church that will eventuate in more writings by talented people. We need a complete new set of hymns. We need to gather small cells of concerned Christians from our communities within our homes and enable them to have prayers, hymns, and Scripture portions in their hands which will serve as stimuli for new, creative, and effective action.

Though I am an urban man and a busy activist, these writings are an attempt to put down prayers on the run. My hope is that they will touch those who have rebelled against the old forms of prayer and worship, or those who have given up on the traditional church. Or perhaps they will help some who have felt guilty about not setting aside a special time for prayer or who have stopped going to a certain place for prayer. May these writings unlock your own creative yearnings and move you to full round-the-clock communion with the One who is the busiest in the midst of life.

1
When You Think You Don't Need Prayer

For many, the idea of prayer is limited to associations with a formal church setting or a time of crisis when the minister or priest is called in to perform his duty of offering "canned" prayers for the occasion. Actually true prayer often is experienced most deeply in those unexpected moments when a flash of insight strikes or that "still small voice" speaks. It may be triggered by a book, a moment of quiet reflection, a memory flashback, or even the anxious anticipation of a very commonplace involvement. Whatever the occasion is, the sad truth is that Mr. Average-Man often thinks that his inarticulate words, his stumbling thoughts, or his non-theological terms cannot reach God. Nothing could be further from the truth. In the Gospels Jesus himself told of some people praying. One of them was an orator who seemed to say just the right thing. He really knew how to impress those about him. There was also another man who, in faltering, hesitating language, said, "God, all I can say is I'm a sinner and need your help!" Jesus held this model prayer up before his disciples and said, "That's the way to pray!"

So these prayers, which are written only to initiate your own prayers, can serve to remind you of something very important: God listens, cares, and responds to all sincere prayer whether offered in church or while on the bus. They are written to kindle moments of prayer in the midst of a busy life. They are written to remind us that some of our most sacred moments may occur during the commonplace minutes of the day when, perhaps, we don't think we really need to pray.

SIDEWALK PRAYER

With the growing urbanization of society, millions of Americans end up in the city or affected by the city's influence. Sitting on a cement bench which bordered the sidewalks of a government center, I could see and hear the people who make up this segment passing by. They were the young college students, the hurrying executives, the busy housewives, the shuffling rejects of the world, and the bent-over elderly; each passing the other on the sidewalk. My prayer came forth this way:

> With tapping feet on concrete walk, my prayer ascends with little talk. Before me spreads the way to song, behind me fall the shadows long, with homes and stores and schools and lawns.
>
> The sidewalk's rolling on and on as weaving thread or binding chain uniting happiness with pain. It links my soul to all mankind, to all caught in the common bind.
>
> O Jesus of the sidewalk way, walk with me through the changing day. Touch each who passes through the hours that they might be as sidewalk flowers.

Good News Shared

As the Father is with me, he is also with you. Cheer up! I have conquered life's problems and so will you! (Based on John 16:32-33.)

WHEN YOU HAVE THE BLAHS

I feel blah, O Jesus! I can't quite put my finger on why but I just don't have the get-up-and-go to make it through the day. I don't go for this religion stuff; and I don't speak any fancy church language. That's why I didn't talk with you before this. But a guy at work noticed how I was acting and he told me that prayer helped him. Can you beat it? I haven't prayed since I was a kid! This guy said that even though things were changing in today's world, prayer is still in. I hope so, because if it isn't, I'm out! I can't lick this by myself. I need you more than I have realized. Fill the emptiness of my life, Lord Jesus, as you seem to have done for my friend. Give me an injection of enthusiasm for life so I'll be worth something. Kick me in the pants if you have to; but help me out!

URBAN SYMPHONY

Scientists tell us that the increase of noises in our urbanized society is deafening mankind. They also are confirmed in their warnings by those who have been fleeing the city to find once again the peace and tranquility of the countryside. Amazingly enough, I have discovered that when you take a group of inner-city children to the country for a vacation, they are frightened and disturbed by the new noises: the crickets, frogs, creaking trees, and whistling wind.

If one listens in the city, he will find that as the rolling hills provide their harmonious sounds, so even the city plays its symphony. Those sounds touch sensitive chords because they are manifesting the movement of all life.

> Drumming of machines, the barking of pets, the squealing of tires, and the roaring of jets; the clanging of bells, the thunder of trains, the harbor tug pulling and grunting in pain—these are the notes of the urban symphony.
>
> The flushing of a toilet and sound of hissing steam, or the rock and roll pounding and the voices that scream; they touch my ears with heightening sensitivity.
>
> The snoring of neighbors and the hawking of wares, or the slamming of doors and the scraping of chairs join little tots' laughter, pigeons flapping by, neighbors out talking, or the little baby's cry; chords of harmony which reach out and touch me.
>
> God be praised for this urban symphony!

Christ Advises Rearrangement

Everyone who decides to be my disciple is like a person who buys a new home; he has to rearrange some of his old furniture and buy some new furniture as well. (Based on Matthew 13:52.)

IN THE KITCHEN

Well, here I am again, Lord, over the dishpan, by the stove, in my kitchen; alone with my thoughts. What will I give the family for supper tonight? A big heavy meal or leftovers? Whatever it is, let your love flow through my fingers, into pots and pans, dishes and foods, into my loved ones.

I feel so guilty when we sit down at the table. I'm tired, unresponsive, and so unable to tell them how much I love and care. So do it for me, will you, Lord? Make them see how beautiful this kitchen has become because you and I have been here so much of the day and because this stove has been an altar where our shared work has become a part of them.

Just keep near me so I'll have patience, understanding, and deeper love—through my kitchen.

Man Calms Plane Passengers

Jesus entered the airplane and his followers went with him. After they took off, the plane ran into a violent storm so that the plane tossed around like a leaf in the air. But Jesus was asleep. One of the men tugged at him and woke him up. "Do something, help us, we're about to crash!" "Calm down," Jesus said, "don't you have any faith at all?" Then he stood in the aisle and looked out the window. They heard him say something and suddenly all was calm. The passengers were amazed. "Who is this guy?" they asked. "Even the winds seem to obey him!" (Based on Matthew 8:23-27.)

IN THE AIR

Seat belts are fastened and we're heading up into the sky, dear Jesus. My heart is beating like a trip-hammer even though I know I'm safer here than in that car on the highway. Calm my fears; turn my attention to the people around me. The stewardess certainly is busy; she takes care of the needs of everyone. Reminds me of the way I think of you; being a person among people; reaching out and helping them as they need help. Thank you, Jesus, for being here so high above the earth, for reaching out, even to me, with tender love. Be in this trip and help me to grow through every one of the experiences before me.

Followers Challenged to Be Different

You've been taught to like the people who are like you and avoid those who are different. But I'm trying to teach you that all people are children of the same God. They all breathe the same air, and are touched by the same sun. So why don't you break loose and get to know them! After all, if you only relate to your friends and family you haven't done much. Even the most limited people do that, and you're supposed to be different! (Based on Matthew 5:43-48.)

ON THE BUS

With a touch of carbon monoxide in the air and a crowd of people all around me, I know I'm a member of the human race; I know I'm one of your children! I'm tempted to withdraw inside and keep these people out. I know I should smile at that man with the long face; even speak to this lady on the seat next to me, but it's hard; they will think I'm kooky.

Lord of buses, cars, and people, flow into these who are here with me. Make me your channel of power. I believe that you are here with us, so show me how I can be more than a pious talker. Make me open to those who are lonely and sad or even happy and glad. Let me affect people so they're better off by being with me.

15

I LOVE TO RIDE THE SUBWAY

Not every city in the United States or Europe has a subway; but certainly the time is not far off when the crowded conditions of earth will force people to travel underground more frequently.

A great portion of my life has been spent traveling the subway. I grew up with it, used it as a means of commuting to school, and lately have used it to get to my office.

One day as I rode the jammed subway train I took out my pad and pencil and wrote the following:

> I love to ride the subway. There's something about the intimacy of the crowds, even the smell of bodies, the swaying of their frames, the uniqueness of clothes, and the variations of hair that fascinate me.
>
> The mystique of strangeness and the unity of mankind overwhelms me like a paradoxical blow of pain and sweetness.
>
> I love the chatter of visiting women and the sports-minded men who share scores of yesterday's events. It all mingles with the click of wheels and squeak of train.
>
> I love to see students clutching their books and cases as though what knowledge they have would somehow escape.
>
> I love to see newspapers waving like sails above the sea of hats. I love to see faces which look like lollipops on sticks, etched with colors of life; some smiling and some frowning.
>
> The darkness of the tunnel engulfs us all. The dim light of bare bulbs casts eerie shadows across multitudes of bodies and we speed on through life toward surfacing and light.

Lawn Provides Lesson

Jesus told a story to his followers about the lawn in the backyard. They didn't quite understand what he meant so he explained it. "The grass seed was put in by the man that is God's Son; the lawn is the world; the good grass is the people who belong to God's kingdom; the crabgrass is the people who follow the evil one; and the guy who put that crabgrass in is the Devil himself. (Based on Matthew 13:37-39.)

IN MY BACKYARD

I'm taking a few moments, Lord, to sit out here and stop everything while the world rushes on. I need these moments to reflect and to talk with you out of the overflow of my heart.

All the things I see around me speak of your presence; the trees, the grass, the flowers, the birds, the clouds above, and even the noises of children, dogs, and busy people. It's funny, but when I'm quiet like this I'm even afraid of the thoughts I'll have. Some people would call them weird but I know you understand me.

Touch me as you touch the earth and make it come alive. Give me new surges of physical strength and inner beauty. Forgive my acting like a machine so much; make me more human, warm, sympathetic, and alive.

DO YOUR THING IN ME, JESUS

Young people talk about doing "their thing." What they mean is that they want to be themselves. Many adults misinterpret "doing your thing" as youth's way of saying they want to live without controls, disciplines, or authority. Nothing could be further from the truth. They want controls with reason, discipline with justice, and authority with love.

The church has let youth down by not relating the "do your thing" thrust to the biblical imperatives which could mean so much to contemporary generations.

The relationship of Jesus Christ to the needs of people today needs to be interpreted in contemporary terms:

> Do your thing in me, Jesus, as you did in Peter; changing a lot of noise into power; forming rock out of sand.
>
> Do your thing in me, Jesus, as you did in Nicodemus; expanding his mind so that a big man became like a little kid; open to all of life!
>
> Do your thing in me, Jesus, as you did in Zacchaeus; stretching a little guy another ten feet, so that stealing and lying were no longer necessary for him.
>
> Do your thing in me, Jesus, as you did in Lazarus. Call me out of the tomb of selfishness and make me alive today!

Teacher Urges People to Be Smart

So, everyone who hears the words I've spoken and does something about them is like the smart contractor who built his skyscraper on a rocky ledge. The water flooded the streets around it and the gales blew, but the building stood because it was built on the rock. (Based on Matthew 7:24-25.)

ON THE WAY TO WORK

Look, God, I'm about to go to work. But I'm really not too anxious. I'd rather be going somewhere else, like to a nice beach, or a show, or out under the green trees. But I've got to go to work and I'm hoping you'll go with me. Kind of give me new strength and a lift so that I can do my best. Help me to face all the unpleasant things as well as to do my best with those people who get under my skin; you know, the petty, jealous, self-centered. OK, I know, I'm that way too; and that's why I'm praying to you—so I won't be. Just stick by, in my words, in my thoughts, in my hands, and in my work; so when the day ends I will know it has been a good day.

Big Invitation Extended

"Here's an invitation," said Jesus, "to all those who are tired of carrying loads of anxieties and burdens of guilt. Take what I have to offer in exchange—forgiveness and love for sin and fear. The burdens you've been carrying are unbearable but what I offer is freedom and joy!" (Based on Matthew 11:28-30.)

IN THE LIVING ROOM

It's great to relax a few minutes, Father, and listen to your still small voice. It tells me you're everywhere; it tells me that you do know even the number of hairs on my head and every one of the prayers I can't even begin to say. Thank you, Father, for life; thank you for permitting me to open my eyes and enjoy again my home and all it means to me.

All around me in this room are things which tell how I've been blessed. The pictures of my loved ones, the little souvenirs I've bought while traveling, the memories associated with each piece of furniture, and even the presence of my friends and family. Man, it's great to be alive! It's wonderful to have a home! It's marvelous to love and be loved! So hear my song of thanks!

The more sobering thoughts of problems, bills, the children, work, health, and taxes come flooding in too. That means I can't go it alone. I need your extra-special lift, God. Give it to me now, so my living room will even become a chapel!

Jesus Explains Kingdom

Finding the kingdom of heaven is like being a shopper who is searching for a string of pearls to give his sweetheart. If he wants the pearls badly enough, he will give up buying other things for himself. He leaves every penny he has in that store in order to buy the pearls. (Based on Matthew 13: 45-46.)

AT THE OFFICE

It's coffee break time, Father, and I've just got to take a few moments to talk with you. There's something about this busyness that frays my nerves; the pressure of getting letters done, files up to date, appointments cleared, and order restored to my desk. Help me to keep cool and patient with myself; to know that there's always another day and especially to know how to keep from losing the best of today.

Forgive me if I've been sharp with those working around me; it's not easy to keep from pettiness and jealousy. But I do want to rise above this and I'm asking you to give me the stuff to be bigger and more mature than I've ever been.

Make me see that those at the desks around me also have their problems. Give me eyes to see their needs and ears to be sensitive to their deeper wants. Make me, in those blue moments, catch the thrill of being part of a team that can even share some of your glory and love.

Jesus Had Problems, Too

Jesus went with his fellow workers, during coffee break, to pray. Alone by himself he prayed, "Father, I've had it. Take this load from me. But, please, God, I'll do what you think is right." (Based on Matthew 26:36-39.)

BEHIND THE MACHINE

Dear Jesus, I'm about to get behind that machine again. Wish I could say I enjoy the monotony of nuts and bolts, put-on, take-off, clatter-clank, sweat, and rumble; I don't. It's a job and I'm doing the best I can to take home a week's pay envelope; but I need your lift. Keep me from falling asleep or getting caught in the machine. But most of all keep me from becoming a dead, automatic part of that machine. Breathe into me new life so I'll be able to see beyond these factory walls and feel as one with all working people. Breathe into me your presence so I'll glow within these factory walls and perhaps weld together those who are here.

2
Lord, Help Me as I Pray

Everyone has his moments of loneliness, depression, guilt, or fear. No matter how busy one may be, there is that inevitable facing of self and all the inner manifestations of turmoil which force us to choose between grinning and bearing it and admitting that we can't go it alone.

The Gospels are full of stories where people cried out to Jesus saying, "Lord, help me!" It wasn't easy for any one of them. They too had to swallow pride and admit weakness; it's probably this fact above all others which keeps people from really praying. No one likes to be thought of as weak or helpless. It seems to be so degrading and even dehumanizing. But if you think about it, we call in the doctor when there is a physical need, or call for the psychiatrist when there is emotional stress, so why not call upon God when one is feeling inadequate? Such calling for help can open up channels of relationship which we may never have known before.

To say, "Lord, help me as I pray," calls for a measure of faith. You have to believe that God can really help. But it's at this point that many give up praying. They find it difficult to believe God is, or that God even cares enough. Jesus was approached by a man who asked his help. When Jesus asked the man if he believed he could help him the man responded, "I believe, but help me when I'm not sure!" Jesus understood this man. He wants honesty; he honors sincerity. He taught his disciples that the doubting man seeking God's help is in better shape than the sure believer who thinks he can go it on his own terms. (This ought to encourage the contemporary, happy pagan who suddenly turns to God with tongue in cheek but still seeking the way!)

ALONE IN THE CROWD

Every time I go into a crowd, whether it's at a football game, in a supermarket, or even in a church, I wonder about the person who feels lonely and unwanted. It doesn't matter how close you are to people, you may still feel terribly isolated from the warmth of friendship and the oneness of humanity. Every one of us has these moments when we sense we are walking through the lonesome valley.

Because we become complete only as we relate to others, there are those who are swallowed up in the lostness of crowded, impersonal living. One day, feeling at one with such people, I wrote the following:

> Hanging on the subway straps we were like sardines in a can. Thousands pass me by each day but nobody takes my hand.
>
> Shoving through the department store, or creeping through the traffic flow, or touching shoulders on the walk, nobody seems to know I'm alive, that I'm a human being or somebody!
>
> Heading for the village or town, while seeking life in the open spaces, I still have an emptiness I find can only be filled by people's faces.
>
> Won't somebody come close to me? Look at me; please! Scream at me, if you must, or beat me, or arrest me! But notice me, will you?
>
> In order to be truly me, I need you!

Hearers Advised to Shine

And Jesus said, "Does anyone ever turn on a lamp in the bedroom and then cover it with a bedspread? Or hide it under the bureau? That's because it's supposed to shine and so are you." (Based on Mark 4:21-23.)

ON GETTING UP IN THE MORNING

It wasn't easy to get out of bed this morning, Lord, but I had to get going. The light seemed to blind my eyes. The thoughts of all the things I have to do seemed to make me more tired; but I know I have you with me. The prospects of another rat race make me weary, so come close to me, Lord, and help me to have that extra strength I need.

My mind is filled with those unfinished tasks. Give me a steadiness and an inner peace, so I'll be able to tick them off one by one. Help me to learn that it's one step at a time; I guess that is what faith is, anyway.

With all the needs there are in the world—people who are looking for a smile to lift them; the lonely who are hoping for the touch of a hand; the hungry who are waiting for the piece of bread—push me in the direction of concern for these people. Then I know my own problems will seem smaller and my own self-pity will die. Fill the day with happiness as I celebrate being alive and share that with others who need me and you.

Picnic Interrupted for Healing

Jesus left the city and tried to have a picnic and a day off in the park. But the word got around and crowds came to see him. They brought the lame, the blind, the crippled, the emotionally disturbed, and all kinds of sick people and insisted he should heal them. He put out his hand and did heal some of them. The newspaper carried the story of this amazing incident. (Based on Matthew 15: 29-31.)

WHILE IN THE HOSPITAL

Good Jesus, you were once called the great physician because you healed people who were sick. I have a doctor whom I trust, but I need more than his medical know-how right now; I need faith and reassurance. I confess I'm scared and weak. No one else knows I'm filled with fear; I know you understand. Put your hand on me as you did to the sick so long ago. Calm my nerves, quiet my fears, deal with my doubts, touch my body.

Be with the nurses, workers, and doctors who work tirelessly in this hospital. Give me understanding of their tiredness from pressures and anxieties too. Help me to smile and be patient. When there is pain, keep me from self-pity and complaints. Deepen my faith so that even death seems insignificant. Make me yours; I need it.

Long-Time Cripple Walks

There is in the capital city a great pool of mineral springs and many sick people come there, hoping to be healed. One man, who had been sick for thirty-eight years, was there and Jesus spotted him. "Would you like to get well?" Jesus asked. The man replied, "You bet I would, but no one will carry me into the pool." Jesus said, "Have faith, get up, and walk." The man did and he was well. (Based on John 5: 1-9.)

BEFORE AN OPERATION

I'm scared, Jesus, so scared! That operation comes soon and I'm scared inside! I've been able to keep it hidden from my family by joking about it, but this operation is no picnic. The pastor came in yesterday and talked about baseball, the weather, my family, and even offered a prayer. I don't think he had any idea how I feel.

That spiritual "Jesus walked the lonesome valley and you must walk it too" comes to my mind. I feel pretty lonesome. I know I have to go through this alone but I guess I'm confessing my need of somebody and that's why I'm turning to you. I learned as a kid that Jesus said he was the shepherd who walked with the sheep in the valley. OK, good Jesus, walk with me through this operation, will you? Take my hand. Change my thoughts. Give me faith. Give me hope. Be with my loved ones so they'll see you with me and discover what I'm discovering, that there's more to it all than this.

Jesus Forgives Woman in Public

Some of the self-righteous church people had pointed the finger at a woman who was an adulteress. But Jesus said, "Which one of you guys has never sinned?" When they didn't answer, he said to the woman, "I don't hold anything against you; go, you are made whole, but try not to sin again." (Based on John 8:3-11.)

WHEN YOU'RE FEELING GUILTY

Look, God, I'm feeling guilty today. Maybe it's because I've had some time to think. Those past mistakes, those things I've done; the things I've said to hurt others, all seem to come in on me and make me feel uncomfortable. I'm not asking you to give me comfort but I know I need to be cleaned, straightened out, and made new. Some call it forgiveness; I call it washing!

I remember reading in the Bible about a man who prayed he would be washed "whiter than snow." Sounds like a commercial but it puts the finger on it.

My problem is not only what I've done, Lord; but also what I haven't done. I know my life doesn't count much for changing this world. I've been so busy taking care of myself and those near me I've forgotten about caring for others, like the poor, the Negro, and the forgotten people who don't live near me. Show me how to make the difference in their lives, too.

IN THE DOCTOR'S OFFICE

Everyone goes to a doctor's office sometime in the course of life. It's usually a time for anxious reflection and personal evaluation. In fact it can be a terribly subjective experience when one's own problems seem to be magnified.

I have a game I play when I'm in a doctor's office. I try to be an artist and paint in my mind the scene I see; the emotions bouncing around become my colors. I also shoot out prayers to the principal actors on the stage of the office and hope they will give some new power to each of them.

One afternoon while waiting patiently to see my doctor I wrote these words:

> It's fun to wait in the doctor's office. The fear of pain, the nagging doubts, and even the lump of guilt seem to sink below the surface.
>
> It's fun to watch the mother with her five children attempting to keep them from open revolt, or the secretary answering the phone and frantically attempting to straighten appointments.
>
> The baby's quick scream from behind the closed door sends a tremor through the nervous patients. The magazine's rattle breaks the heaviness of the quiet like a machine gun in the night.
>
> The red-faced, blustering, fat man asks why the doctor is so long. The answer: "He's been at the hospital setting bones from an accident."
>
> The old man huddles in his chair, clutching his cane as though it is an anchor of security.
>
> The phone rings and everyone jumps again. They finally enter the door of hope and night falls again.
>
> The office is empty; all that remains are the sighs, moans, laughs, and groans.

Jesus Says There's No Need to Worry

Don't get yourself all upset always worrying about future events. God knows what your needs are and he will take care of you. Invest your life in service to others and a lot of these things will straighten themselves out. (Based on Luke 12:29-31.)

WHEN YOU ARE WORRIED

The worries have got me down, O Lord, pick me up! They're all real: the bills, the family, the health problems, the job pressures, the mess our country's in—they all are pressing in on me. Then, there's Bill in the army; what if he gets killed? There's Susan at college; you hear about dope and pregnancies. There's Roger's little girl; will she need an operation? God, these are more than I can stand. They follow me day and night.

I remember that book I read on worry which said we can't all play God and solve the world's problems. I know that's what I do. Can't help it; that's the way I am. Change my ways, will you? What I need is a greater trust in you and perhaps greater trust of others. I should have learned by now; my past worries weren't necessary. So calm my fears; remind me of these positive things. Replace my worries with simple faith. Thank you, Jesus.

Son Welcomed Back

The son who had left home was greeted by his father while he was still way down the street. His father ran to him, threw his arms around him, and kissed him. The boy said, "Dad, I've been pretty rotten with you and with God. I'm not fit to be called your son." But the father forgave him and forgot all his son had done, and they celebrated his return. (Based on Luke 15:20-24.)

WHEN YOU CAN'T STAND YOURSELF

I'm looking in the mirror, Jesus, and I can't stand what I see. I wish I were somebody else, with a better looking face, better body, bigger mind, and more successful life.

Wonder how you put up with characters like me? But then, I remember that's just what you did, didn't you? There were some strange people in your crowd: smelly fishermen, crooked politicians, prostitutes, pious churchmen, conniving opportunists! As I think of it, there aren't many people who are very lovely, and yet you seem to accept them all. That's what I'm needing; to be accepted by you. Somehow to know of your love helps me to accept myself.

Funny, as I stand here looking in my mirror and talking to you, I want to laugh. That's what you want me to do, don't you? Laugh at myself so I can be down to earth like you. OK, I admit it is funny for me to be whining and griping when there are so many others who have greater needs. Some of us do look ridiculous refusing to accept ourselves when you do. I'm laughing, Jesus, with you!

Jesus Offers New Kind of Water

Jesus said to the woman at the drinking fountain in the center of the town of Samaria, "If you knew who I really am and what I have to offer you, you would ask me for it. You see, I have a new kind of water and all you need to do is ask and it is yours." (Based on John 4:10.)

FOR A RAINY DAY

It's raining outside, O Lord, and I'm in no mood for singing about the showers of blessings! This kind of day gets under my skin. I feel all gray inside and want to rise above the darkness of the clouds. I know we need the rain for the grass and trees and I also know you can't have lakes and streams without the rain; but right now my biggest problem, I guess, is my own need of refreshing water and life-giving streams.

Help me as I look at the rain to open my soul to your waters of life. Give me positive thoughts, bright ideas, new goals, and concern for others. As trees can't duck the rain, help me to remember that I can't flee from the unpleasant things of life. Strengthen me with new willpower and faith through Him who is the water of life.

3
Church Activists Need Prayer Too

Church activists need prayer more than anybody else because there is something about being involved in church affairs that builds an insular coating around a person. Perhaps it's because he has usually worked out his creeds and doctrines; maybe it's because he's convinced that his activity is proof of his being within God's will. But close scrutiny of the teachings of Jesus shows that there is a devastating danger facing such activists; it is the failure to stop long enough to listen to the whisper of God. So many of us are so busy running about that when it comes to spiritual power we find we're running out!

The poem "On the City Street" was written when I had slipped away to a church conference and had an opportunity to look at myself quietly and evaluate what I was doing through the church. The poor and burdened of the city entered the hallways of my mind and banged on the doors. They had a message for us busy, middle-class, pious church people. They wanted to make me aware of their praying, too; they were praying for me inside that church building! They were praying I'd have new eyes to see and new ears to hear!

Prayers by men like Carl Burke or Malcolm Boyd may shake up the traditionalists, but generally such prayers simply don't appeal to a lot of people. We need more than the language of the reform school or the nightclub; we need to build upon what is familiar and emotionally significant for the church worker, and at the same time add new, contemporary dimensions which will hasten his tuning in to God.

THE CHURCH OVER THERE

The frequent speaking engagements I have take me into numbers of cities and towns where I have opportunity to see churches on a Sunday morning. There always seem to be two parades; those going into the church buildings and those passing by.

It was while I was in London that I saw a clergyman in flowing gowns walk from his nearby vicarage to the church. A number of poor, cockney children brushed by him and he seemed oblivious to them; he still must have been working on that sermon!

I saw myself suddenly as the busy, pious, praying church-man of the church and wrote "On the City Street":

> That's the church over there. I see people going in; nicely dressed, well fed, fat, and comfortable.
>
> That's the church over there. I hear music through the windows; hymns, choirs, organ, and voices.
>
> That's the church over there. I see clergy slipping in the door; busy, pious, holy, and clean.
>
> But, I'm over here; smashed, angry, little, and bleeding!
>
> The music I hear is screaming, cursing, hate, and filth! My doorway has gum wrappers, beer bottles, stink, and kids! Besides, it's shut so the drunk can sleep and the woman can hide.
>
> That's the church over there; but I'm over here! I'm lonely, beaten, trapped, and shot!
>
> Man, what's the church doing over there?

Nazarene Holds Up Love

The clergy tried to trap Jesus with the question, "Which is the most important teaching in the church?" Jesus answered, "The first is to love the Lord, your God, and the second is to love your neighbor as much as you love yourself." (Based on Matthew 22:34-39.)

BEFORE THE CHURCH SERVICE

Lord of all people everywhere, that Sunday hour of worship has arrived. I'm going to be there because I think the kids need it; but I'll confess I'd rather stay in bed or head for the golf course. You're right. I need it too: the chance to be quiet; the chance to think; the chance to be with other people who admit they're as sinful as I am—they're all mine today.

When I sit in that pew, stimulate me so I won't sleep. Let me be alert to all that's happening. Give me understanding of those hymns with the old-fashioned words and those prayers that sometimes seem to leave me cold. Yes, open me up so I'll be able to be myself; relaxed about my weak spots and tense over the needs of the world. Be with the man in the pulpit. Let him know that I'm pulling for him and you're pushing him. Give him the guts to speak like a prophet of old and I'll back him up all the way.

Speaker Hits Religious Leaders

Watch the ministers and priests, even though they represent the church. They may be preaching and teaching the right things but be careful of living like them. They do not practice what they preach! (Based on Matthew 23:1-3.)

FOR THE RELIGIOUS LEADER

I've been trying all week, Lord God, to get myself in shape for this worship service and now that it's here I don't feel up to it. I feel inadequate; probably because I'm standing in your place, speaking your words. You know how I love to hear the organ play, to see the people before me, to sense my part in shaping the lives of these people. Keep me from being so caught up with the importance of my job that I don't deal with its realities. Give me the courage to speak the truth in love, to love those who disagree with me, and to work with those who don't want to work. Give me the patience to put up with pettiness and jealousy just as you have done through all the years. And help me to keep my sense of humor so I can laugh at myself when necessary and laugh at others when it's the right time. Push me out into the world, even when I would prefer to remain in my study; and fill me with fire that your will might burn its way through hard hearts.

36

THE BOMBED CATHEDRAL

Hundreds of tourists, from all over the world, visit the bombed, scarred Cathedral of Coventry in England. It stands as a testimony to the careless ravages of war and man's capacity to love in the midst of hate.

It was a fascinating experience to wander amongst the ruins, to see the charred cross on the altar open to the sky. It was especially inspiring to see the new cathedral adjacent and to learn of its contemporary shape of ministry.

I sat on a cement bench and wrote "In Coventry Cathedral":

> I stood in a cathedral which was laid in ruins by the bombs of angry men. I saw the scars of stupidity which served as altars to technology. I felt the foolishness of hatred as we fought a war again.
>
> I stood in a cathedral open to sky and wind and sun; open to the sounds of city and the movement of humanity. They thought it was crushed never to rise again but it was alive, and vibrant in its pain.
>
> I stood in a cathedral with doors forced open, with stained glass gone, with altar splintered and its cross on fire.
>
> The city now pours through its body. Cries of despair still echo through its stones. Songs of hope reverberate to the spire. A scrawny sparrow invades its heart. An old man sits on its pocked steps. Two lovers seek a shadowed corner. Children scamper through its windows and a stray dog nuzzles my hand. He even seems glad he can stand by me in the ruined cathedral!

Teacher Upset with Woman

Salome, the mother of James and John, visited Jesus and asked him to give her sons a special place in his kingdom. But Jesus was upset. "Leadership and rewards are earned," he said. "The most important thing is not how successful they are but what they do with their lives; can they live by the will of my Father?" (Based on Matthew 20:20-23.)

FOR THE ACTIVE CHURCHWOMAN

Well, Jesus, I'm about to plunge into the usual routine at the church: make the list, phone the gals, check the details, prepare the devotions, bake a cake, pick up Joan, and go to more meetings. I sometimes wonder if it's all worth it? Is this really the way you want us to spend our time? There are times when I want to chuck it all and then I think of how we do get some things done. In spite of our spending so much time on talk we are making some progress. Anyway, Master, I've got to believe that, so help me to know, will you?

Maybe what I need today is inspiration so I'll bring freshness to my own women's group. Maybe what I need is to change my own ways so I'll start in new directions other than just turning the same old wheels. Maybe we haven't been very imaginative or daring; so give us some leads, Jesus, on how to really reach out into this community; how to really make the difference in lifting the poor, giving dignity to the black, and bringing others closer to you. Help us to see that what counts is more than rolling bandages and serving suppers; we want to be instruments of change in your world.

Five Local Girls Miss Wedding

There was a great wedding celebration. Ten girls went to it by bus. When they were about to board, five of them discovered they had forgotten to take money with them. They thought they could borrow from the other girls, but the others had no extra change. So the five foolish girls, without money, missed arriving at the wedding party. (Based on Matthew 25:1-10.)

AT THE YOUTH MEETING

Here we are gathered, good Jesus, at another youth meeting. Sometimes it seems that we're dead inside when we get together like this; it all seems like sham and hypocrisy. But that's why we're here—to do something about it. So, come on, get close to us and let's really go somewhere!

We don't want to spend our time on the small stuff! With war all around us give us sense enough to see how to be peacemakers and guts enough to dare to try! With prejudice all around us, give us color blindness so we'll do something about prejudice against the Negro, the Mexican, the Indian, and others, and love enough to stand by our convictions! With deprivation all around us, make us uncomfortable about our own affluence and help us to understand how to change systems which breed poverty. With moral standards crashing, help us to have mature dealings with sex, so we'll hurt no one and will be able to be models of clean living.

So, Jesus, this is why we're here; not to blame others for the world we live in but to find out how we can reshape it as you would like it done.

FROM THE PULPIT CHAIR

Do church people, or even those who have given up on the church, ever wonder what goes through the mind of a clergyman as he sits in the chancel and looks down upon a congregation? One Sunday while visiting a church as guest preacher I looked down at the people and felt like getting up and running. However, I fought the impulse and, after the service and its handshakes, I went to the study and recorded my feelings.

Some might say this makes good case study material. But I have the feeling it expresses an occasional mood which grips the man of the cloth. Why do I include it here? Because it will help some to pray more intelligently for him.

> The moon faces rise with the opening hymn. Caverns yawn, jowls bulge, lips smack, teeth click, and words dance as we sing together.
>
> Before me is a sea of faces, faces, faces. They hide behind bunkers, fortresses, and shields called hymnbooks.
>
> The doxology, gloria, and amens lead to offering, sermon, and then—the word of Christ for all men!
>
> God is here! The word is alive. But eyeballs roll, mouths purse, pulses beat, and pressures rise. There are stone faces, cruel faces, and dead faces!
>
> My God, get me out of here! I want to run, run, run! I want to flee, flee, flee! I want to die!
>
> Hide me in a hole, O God! Zip me up; I can't take anymore!
>
> Strip off my robe; help me slip away fast.
>
> Oh, God, our help in ages past, do you know what I'm saying?
>
> Get me out of here; away from stained glass, incense, and cold candles!

Church Leader Challenged

There was a leading church-man named Nicodemus who came during the night to ask questions of Jesus. "We know you have special gifts from God; how can we do the great things you're doing?" he said to him. "Well," replied Jesus, "why don't you try being born all over again—that's what you need." (Based on John 3:1-5.)

THE CHURCH EXECUTIVE'S PRAYER

Divine Leader of men, I remember Nicodemus' searching questions when he visited you. He must have felt terribly inadequate after listening to your teaching and observing your miracles, and so do I! All of my years of experience in the church and I still know I have not measured up to the position I've attained. Forgive me; show me how to find my own rebirth of spirit.

Send me back to those glowing days of discovery when I was more naïve than now, but perhaps closer to you. Help me to begin over again with a simple faith and a warm love. It's so easy to develop the executive stare, looking beyond people, or to be caught up in the rush of turning the wheels of church machinery and losing humanity. Make me human, O Jesus.

As I move from desk to altar and from pulpit to planes, give me the steadiness of spirit and openness of mind that will keep me growing. May the interests of the whole church be mine; lift me above my own brand of sectarianism into dynamic ecumenism. Most of all keep me in touch with the poor, the angry, the lonely, the forgotten; so I'll be in touch with you.

41

4
Pray for the Other Guy

There is much talk about a generation gap today. But I think there are actually generation "gaps." There's the gap between children and adults; there's the gap between youth and adults; and there's even a greater gap between the middle-aged and those who are over sixty-five—to say nothing of the gaps between the black and white, and the middle-class straight and the so-called "hippie"!

Prayer is one way to overcome gaps. If people can earnestly pray for those who are different from themselves, they will be required to precede and follow that praying with openness, sensitivity, and understanding. How often are prayers offered on behalf of the black man who demands just reparations? How often are prayers uttered on behalf of the long-haired, bearded youth who repulses the outwardly clean middle-class American? How often is the cry of our youth incorporated into an articulate expression of prayer for wisdom and responsiveness?

For ten years I served virile churches in the Midwest. One institution which still went strong in those churches was the midweek prayer service. But, I must confess, our custom of praying for others was limited primarily to a list of the hospitalized and the shut-ins. Since then, as I have visited churches of all denominations even during the regular Sunday morning worship service, I have noticed an increasing tendency to mention the sick from the pulpit, and to offer a prayer on their behalf. This is great and it ought to be continued; but what of those who are well but alienated? What of those who are strong but lonely because of age differential? What of those who are trapped in the ghetto because of their skin color? Perhaps one reason we don't get stirred to action on their behalf is that we have forgotten them in our praying.

Prophet Welcomes Kids

Some people brought kids to Jesus hoping he'd give them some special blessing, but the disciples were upset with those people for trying to make a showman out of the Master. Jesus spoke to those disciples and said, "Let the kids come, because they're the ones I'm concerned about; I've got something they need." Then he put his hands on the little ones and left. (Based on Matthew 19: 13-15.)

FOR THE KIDS

I've seen that picture of you holding the little children on your lap, good Jesus. They were all colors and all kinds. I have some kids of my own and also some memories of what it was like to be a child. So put your hand out and bless them, just as you did in that story in the Bible.

As fathers and mothers, a lot of us are troubled by the kind of world we're bringing these kids up in. It's full of hatred and violence; it's preoccupied with smut and filth; it's loaded with litter and rubbish. Help us to find ways to make it beautiful and good. Give us the eyes to see the things that will enrich these kids and give us the guts to teach the values that will stand by them. Most of all, Jesus, give us the strength to live the kind of lives that will inspire them to be noble. Teach them, through us, to love each other, whether black, brown, red, yellow, or white, as you also love them.

AN OPEN LETTER TO MOM AND DAD

There's a revolution going on and it's being carried out by the younger generation. It baffles and frightens middle-agers who find it difficult to understand what it's all about.

A great deal of my time has been spent attempting to relate the church and the adult world to the contemporary youth culture. What I have discovered is a deep religious sensitivity on the part of youth to the world's needs. They have not turned off the church; but they have rejected all that is phony in church people.

I believe in our youth! I believe they are taking seriously what we taught so lightheartedly. This cry is my effort to communicate, all too imperfectly, what I've heard them say:

> They talk about the generation gap and wonder what's happening to us. But who's listening to our cry as we try to explain?
>
> You taught me at home, "blessed are the pure in heart"; but drugs and your example blew that apart!
>
> You taught me in school, "one nation with liberty for all"; but the black man's lot proves he's got a long haul!
>
> You taught me in scouts, "trustworthy and loyal" is the code; but your business ventures went another road!
>
> You taught me in Sunday school the poor in spirit the kingdom brings; but all you really want is things and more things!
>
> O Christ of the pure in heart, the poor, and hungry, the crooked and false, and the misguided pious; I'm not blaming anyone, but this is my world! I want to put it back together again! Who will help me do it?

IN HER ROCKING CHAIR

Once in a while a person writes something as though he were an artist attempting to put on canvas a picture which he has in his soul. My "little old lady" in the rocking chair is such a painting. She typifies the increasing numbers of elderly who can no longer warm pews or even fill their offering envelopes. But they are the lonesome millions who are forced to live with their memories and rock to their own tunes. Perhaps this writing will trigger the memory machine of some grandmother; or perhaps it will motivate a concerned adult to make that visit or phone call.

> She's a little old lady in faded shawl, alone in her room at the end of the hall, rhythmically moving her rocking chair, hypnotized by the memories there. There's Charlie's popped question and Billie's first tooth; or Cathy's broken leg and Peggy's telling the truth. There's the shiny first car or the operation on the ear; the pressures of studies and the high spots of cheer. Then the hymns in the church and the preachers now gone; the thrilling baptisms and Easters at dawn. Or neighbors at lunch and games to play; the sadness of death and neighbors that stay.
>
> She's a little old lady in faded shawl with a little room at the end of the hall filled with figures and faces of loved ones and friends and memories and prayers that will never end.

Old Man Made to See

They took the man who used to be blind to the minister at the church and said, "Jesus claimed to make this man see, and it was even a Sunday. How could anyone cure a blind man who didn't obey all the church laws?" The man who had been blind said, "I don't know about that but I know one thing—now I can really see." (Based on John 9:13-16.)

ON BEHALF OF THE SENIOR MEMBERS OF SOCIETY

O Friend of the young and old alike, hear my prayer for the aging in my home or the community around me. I confess I do not understand them at times—their childishness or reminiscing; their set ways and conservatism—but I pray for better understanding that I may be more thoughtful and sensitive to their ways and needs. I'm sure I have no concept of their loneliness; so many of their friends have moved away or died. Let me fill the vacuum when the opportunity arises. I'm certain I cannot feel their aches and pains; let me offer the hand of love when it's needed most. Help me to say the right words, offer the right counsel, and live in the best attitude as I too prepare myself for entrance into the mysteries of aging.

Child Healed at Distance

Jesus went into the suburbs of Tyre and Sidon. A woman who lived there came to him and asked him to cure her daughter who was ill at home. The disciples asked Jesus to get rid of her because she was a nuisance. But Jesus made it clear that this was the reason he had come to earth. The woman fell at his feet while he was having coffee and said, "Please help me!" Then he said to her, "You are a woman of great faith," and word came later that at that moment her daughter was healed. (Based on Matthew 15:21-28.)

FOR A SICK FRIEND

Dear Lord, friend of the sick and suffering, today I want to remind you of the needs of my friend. I know you are aware of my friend's needs even before I mention them, but I guess I have to talk to you about them in order to increase my own faith and because I believe my faith and love truly affects them. I'm not asking for any special miracles, even though I might really hope for one, except the miracle of your presence and peace. I pray that my friend will know you are there with outstretched hand, surging power, and lifting love. Give new hope and new life, we pray, in your Son's name.

Disturbed Man Interrupts Service

Jesus was acting as guest preacher in the little town of Capernaum. During the service a mentally disturbed man interrupted the worship by standing up and shouting at Jesus. Instead of berating him the Master looked upon him with love and understanding. He quietly asked the man to calm down and be relaxed. Then he asked that the man be made whole. The fellow screamed and then became quiet. The people marveled and the news spread that Jesus had healed a mental patient. (Based on Mark 1:21-28.)

FOR THE MENTALLY ILL

O Jesus, you stand out among all people as being emotionally mature; the one who enters into the lives of the disturbed to bring peace and tranquillity. As you touched the mentally ill and helped them to return to reality, so touch the troubled person I am thinking of with your steadying, healing power. If there is deep unconscious guilt, may it be lifted out. If there is stunted emotional growth, may new growth take place. If there is fear of people who make one feel small and inadequate, build the bridges of love and trust so that wholeness may take place.

We are all mystified by emotional illness. Open our eyes so we'll accept it as we accept physical disease. Teach us more; release our faith. Help us to learn from each other that we may discover the key to mature living.

TRY BEING HUMAN

Two explosions have changed the world; the population explosion and the technological explosion have tended to bury people as human beings. The growing masses and the rapid mobility have made it difficult to relate to people except as consumers, passengers, or social security numbers.

The church is one of the few institutions left that says its main business is to help individuals relate to individuals. That means that real prayer also seeks to bring out the humanity within us. It seeks to relate us as people to persons who seek love and understanding.

> Try joining the human race . . . today that guy over there needs you . . . slip under his skin . . . look into his eyes . . . probe into his words . . . shove into his shoes . . . feel the pain . . . note the lumps . . . grab the him . . . shoot smiles into his clouds . . . zip prayers into his soul . . . paint hope on the walls of his mind . . . join the human race . . . today!

BUT THEN, HE'S A HIPPIE

People in the building where I worked were always somewhat shocked by the long-haired, bearded youths who entered my office. After all we were the well-groomed, middle-class establishment who had forgotten that the same rights we had fought for in order that a black man might be accepted as a person applied to the one who refused to cut his hair or wear standard, middle-class clothing.

One summer day I sat at a sidewalk cafe with a hippie and another churchman. It was amazing to see people do a double take as they tried to figure out why two square, business-suited men should be hobnobbing with this youth. The experience so affected me I had to put this down on paper:

> Did you ever eat at a sidewalk cafe with a hippie? I did; it's like being with a leper. People make sudden turns and stare with disbelieving eyes. They shake their heads and rejoice that they're not like him. It's funny; he talks like them and thinks like them. Only his talk is deeper and more profoundly spiritual. His thoughts are high and they're full of concern for others—but then, he's a hippie!
>
> What makes him different? Is it his hair? George Washington had hair like that; he too talked about freedom for all men! Is it his beard? Abe Lincoln had a beard like that and healed a whole nation. Is it his bell-bottomed pants? Sailors still wear them and they guard our shores with honor. Is it his dirt? The fishermen of Galilee couldn't have been dirtier, yet they changed the course of the world. Is it his sandals? Monks wear them while their prayers move the church.
>
> What's the problem then? Well, a hippie's different, that's all!
>
> Oh, yes, and so was another man with beard and hair, and Nazarene dress, fishy smell, and sandals too—and they crucified him!

Jesus Likes Hippies

You religious people claim to be spiritual. Some of you think religion should be gloomy, tough, unhappy. That's the way John the Baptist was, and you cut him off. Then I came with joy and humaneness, and you accused me of being a glutton and a drunk. You pointed at me and said, "Look, there's proof, he spends his time with crooks and hippies." But I have news for you: these lowly people have the real joy and the real power. (Based on Matthew 11:16-19.)

FOR THE HIPPIE

Those kids are different, Jesus, and I must admit I just don't like to see beards, long hair, and all that jewelry. I suppose it's because they dare to be different that I get upset; maybe they make me unconsciously wish I could break out of the mold and be myself. But anyway, give me understanding of what they say and how they live. Make me see the positive aspects of what they represent; like refusing to bet their lives on middle-class values which put money and things at the center of life. Just as you saw beyond the outward dress of smelly fishermen in Galilee and prostitute women who were condemned by the church leaders of your time, so give me the ability to see these kids as human beings who are trying to say something to the world. Since I'm that world, I really need to listen and learn.

BLACK IS BEAUTIFUL

It took a long time for the church to discover that they had
made black an ugly, evil, devilish color. We use terms like
"black Friday," "blacklist," "blackball," and we drape our
altars in black as the symbol of death and finality. No wonder
the black man tried to deny his blackness; but things have
changed and the black man has helped us whites to see that
black is truly beautiful!

One runs a risk in attempting to write about blacks or
even their blackness because we touch chords related to the
gap between blacks and whites. However, this writing has
been read by some of my black friends and, with their ap-
proval, I put it down recognizing that it can never measure
up to the black man's own expression of the same truth:

> Black is beautiful! It fills the sky so stars stand
> out; it penetrates rocks with magical brush; it
> tinges clouds while sprinkling the earth.
> Black is beautiful! It carpets streets and shining
> shoes; it saturates furs with glossy sweep; it tinges
> ocean depths below and even hallows clerical
> robes.
> Black is beautiful through shining faces of African
> strand; etched with strength from slavery and tears.
> They throw back shoulders with pride and glow
> for conquests made through suffering years. They
> speak of freedom and newfound power; the beau-
> tiful black has reached his hour!

Christ Assails Racists

How terrible for you so-called religious people! You are fakes! You give your money for missions but you neglect the most important religious rule, which is fighting for justice, demonstrating mercy, and being honest about things. (Based on Matthew 23:23-24.)

FOR THE BLACK MAN

I've been watching television, O Christ, and I can't express the revulsion I feel at learning about some of the things we have done to the black man: like the way we've degraded him for 200 years; the destruction of his pride and person; the horrible things we've done through lynching, bombing, shooting, and apathetic indifference. How you must have anguished over this while we insisted it wasn't all that bad. Forgive us, O Christ, and be with the black man. Give him pride in his blackness, dignity in his time of revolution, and friends, like me, who will confront the systems and people that have continued to do this.

Free him from justified hatred. Free him from legitimate prejudice. Free him from violence by altering the political and economic systems which I have perpetuated without thinking. Continue to give him a song to sing and a happiness to share with the awareness that you and I are with him and the victory will come.

Jesus Predicts His Own Death

As Jesus was going up to Jerusalem he took the twelve disciples aside and said, "Listen, we're going up to the city of Jerusalem where there's a gang of officials waiting to kill me. They will rig a trial, go through the motions of justice, make a public spectacle of me, and finally kill me; but three days later they will discover I can't be destroyed. I will be alive." (Based on Matthew 20: 17-19.)

FOR THE MOURNING FAMILY

Lord of life and death, I've just received word of the sudden death of my friend's son. What a shock it is; he's cut off from life so soon and his wife and children are stunned by it all. O Jesus, it's at moments like this that all the little, insignificant things of life show up in their true perspective. We see the real things that matter when we face death. We even ask what life is all about and question whether or not we are ready to leave it.

I'm sure you understand what I'm trying to say because you've been through it and you've died the death of agony. I confess I don't quite understand this resurrection bit; but then, who does? Somehow, even though I don't understand, I believe it. May my friend and his family also believe it. May they feel you near and feel comforted because you've been through it too. May their faith be helped and their tears be dried by the awareness of my love and yours. Most of all, may they somehow see beyond death into the new horizon of hope.

5
Prayer Can Saturate Life

Prayer is more than a Sunday exercise; it is a constant aware-ness of the presence of God in all of life. A story out of Paris claims that Voltaire, the professed atheist, once tipped his hat toward a crucifix as it was carried by in a religious procession. When a friend questioned him about his action he said, "We salute but we do not speak." For many, their relationship to God is tipping the hat but not including him in all of life's moments.

As one reads the story of Jesus' life in the Gospels, the importance of prayer to all Jesus did is obvious. He got up early in the morning and went into a quiet place to pray. His teachings breathed the presence of God in them. His friend-ship with all people, including the fishermen, the sanctimoni-ous religious leaders, the crude politicians, and the vile lepers, was shot through with compassion, outflow of love, concern for personhood, and forgiving; this is prayer-satura-tion at its best.

It was said that a friend of St. Francis eavesdropped during his prayer time with the hope of discovering the technique for true power-filled praying. All he heard was, "My God, my God, my God" and this went on all night long. Prayer may be just that simple. One may walk the sidewalks or ride the bus and sing the constant song in his heart, "My God, my God, my God." Think what would happen in the midst of strained family relationships, or when communities are torn apart by class and race hatred, or when problems are about to smack us if we sensed that God is really nearer than hands or feet, closer than breath or life!

THE SKYSCRAPER

Skyscrapers have always intrigued me. They do to me what mountains do; they inspire and fill me with awe. So they are man-made. What difference does it make? God still gave man the technological know-how, the materials, and the drive. So, in fact, high buildings become the mountaintops of urban society and seen in that light they may even point us to the Creator and Redeemer of all.

One day, seated at the foot of one of these buildings in the heart of the city, I wrote the following:

> Concrete beauty stretching high, man-made mountain reaching for the sky, fifty-two stories of aluminum and glass, you're circled by concrete, trees, and grass.
>
> Some scorn you for your frightening height. Some hate you for your ugly sight. I see God in your lines and form as I see God in the fields of corn.
>
> Gleaming white structure piercing the blue, above an old city, shiny and new; you lift little people above the street and give to children a view and treat.
>
> Some climb you just because you're there. Others climb you to sense pure air. But I climb you to contemplate the day and to see again the Higher Way.

Four Thousand Fed

Jesus called his disciples together and said: "I feel sorry for these people; they're hungry. Let's feed them." The disciples said, "Where will you find any food? There's no store or restaurant around here." But Jesus said, "You all have some lunches, share those." So the fishermen shared their lunches and a miracle took place. There was enough to feed four thousand men plus women and children. (Based on Matthew 15:32-37.)

AT THE TABLE

We hold hands around this table, dear Lord, to remind ourselves of the hands that have made this food possible:

Your hand, which is always moving over the earth, as sun and rain and life;

The farmer's hand, which sows the seed, runs the machines, and sends the food to factories;

The trucker's hand which loads the grain, carries the meat, distributes the vegetables;

The laborer's hand at the factory, which packs the cereal, washes the vegetables, prepares the meat;

The grocer's hand, which makes this available to us;

Then there's Mom's hand which has cooked and prepared this meal.

For all these hands we give you thanks.

May our hands be strengthened in love so they can reach out to others as others have reached to us.

Faith Is the Thing

Let me tell you what the kingdom of God is really like. See that acorn, it is small, and it fell from the tree by the sidewalk. Out of it will come a big oak tree; that is if you'll plant it with faith and tender care. (Based on Mark 4:30-32.)

BEFORE SHOPPING

I've got to get down to the store, O Jesus, but I want to stop briefly to ask you to go with me. You don't know what it means for me to feel I'm not alone in all this. I don't have enough money to buy all I want and yet I know I have a lot more than some do. I'm not complaining, Lord, just asking you to keep me sharp and alert, so I'll buy wisely and thoughtfully.

There are times when I'm shopping that it seems to be the same old thing; what will I buy for meals? How far can I go with this money? What can I do to squeeze out enough for shoes for the children? Sometimes I get angry and impatient because of the boredom and because I feel inadequate to make some of the decisions.

Perhaps by being sensitive to other shoppers, clerks, and lonely strangers I'll find this is more than a shopping tour. Maybe I'll come back a better person because I've thought of more than food, money, and clothes. I hope so—that's why I'm counting on you.

Evening Miracle Takes Place

When evening came and the sun had set, people brought to Jesus others who were sick of body and mind. And Jesus healed many of these folk, giving them new health and a new peace. (Based on Mark 1:32-34.)

BEFORE GOING TO BED

Jesus of the day and night, draw close to me and my loved ones as we get ready for bed. It's been a hard, tiring day and I'm not sure even sleep will help. In fact I'm not even certain I can sleep without pills, so I'm turning to you. There have been times in the lives of others when you've been so near and real that peace and calm came to them. I guess I'm asking you to do the same for me. Touch my body so it will relax; I'm relaxed, Lord. Touch my soul so it will be filled with your peace; I have your peace, Lord. Touch my mind so I'll stop worrying about things and slip off into the unconscious; I give my mind over to you, Lord. Wake me and my family with freshness and new life; I believe, Lord Jesus.

THE REVOLVING DOOR

How we take for granted the symbols of urban life. We've been reared to appreciate the barn, the plow, the scarecrow, the haystack, and the stone wall; but what about the fire station, the corner store, the department store, or the revolving door? The latter has always intrigued me. Perhaps it will be gone one day; perhaps it will be completely replaced by the electronic eye; but it still stands as a symbol with meaning. See what you think.

> Pushing on the revolving door, I join crowds quickly passing through. They dramatize the flow of life, passing from old to new.
>
> There's the mother with her little boy; break the grip, do it alone. There's the lover with his only love; loosen the hands; push the load. Jabbering salesgirls leave for lunch, "See you later on the other side." A gang of boys with jingling coins come seeking sights and treasures too. An old man on wobbly cane pushes painfully toward his goal.
>
> Some push at the revolving door, never thinking as they spin. Others enter it anticipating surprises as they slip right in.

Eternal Life Promised

Listen to my voice like a pet listens to the voice of its master. He knows what's best for it as I know what's best for you. I promise you eternal life; you shall never die; and no one can change that. (Based on John 10:27-28.)

THE SENIOR CITIZEN'S PRAYER

God who made me so long ago and who has continued to give me the breath of life, hear my humble and simple prayer as I greet another day. My body isn't what it used to be; give me the strength to rise above its weakness. My mind slips occasionally; give me the keenness to maintain thought and memory. Keep me from dying in mind and spirit. Help me to grow till the last breath leaves my body, and then help me to still grow. I confess my sin and even my unpreparedness for death; be at my side that I may be ready. May I leave a heritage of joy, friendship, love, and harmony with those I leave behind. But in the meantime show me how I can be useful even in limited ways to your honor and glory.

A New Rule for Life Presented

You have heard it said, an eye for an eye and a tooth for a tooth, but listen to me, don't practice revenge! If someone cuts in front of you in a car, don't cut back! (Based on Matthew 5:38-39.)

BEFORE DRIVING IN THE CAR

I haven't done much praying about my driving, Jesus, but I do want you to hear me now. I'll be out in that car, heading down the road, and I need you with me—not as a rabbit's foot but as the breath of sanity which helps me to drive like a human being. We all know 50,000 people die in cars every year, Jesus, but we never believe it can happen to us. So maybe I need to be scared a little—for myself, my family, and those strangers I will pass on the road. Give me steadiness of hand, an alert mind, a sensitivity for others, and cool emotions. Keep me from taking chances or forgetting to do the right things in times of emergency. Most of all, may my thoughts be so tuned to you that everything I do while behind that wheel will be pleasing to you and bring greater safety to our highways and roads.

6
Wake Up the Church, Jesus

The church is under fire these days. There are those, especially among the younger set, who believe the church has
lost its thrust because it's lost its nerve. Running the risk of
oversimplification, I would be more inclined to say it has
lost its thrust and its nerve because it has given up praying!
It has succumbed to the sophisticated brainwashing of a technological age which regards prayer as being a piety hangover
from the agricultural age. Perhaps there is some truth in this
attitude; more certainly the maintenance of the nineteenth-
century language and rural imagery has played a great part
in this new hesitance to talk about prayer or to admit it's
necessary.

The average worship service is still steeped in lifeless litany and unexciting hymnology. The minister or priest seems
to grind out the phrases and mumble the words as though
Christendom is a thing of the past and an embarrassment of
the present.

Not every church needs to fire its organist and hire a
guitarist! Not every church needs to scrap its litany and pick
up what is strange and foreign. But almost every church
needs to be awakened with new, fresh words, and new re-
vitalized prayers, accompanied by familiar music which has
words related to the issues of life.

I believe in the church; but if it is to be made dynamic and
relevant it has to start among "the gathered"! It has to awak-
en through combined action and prayer!

It's Dignity that Counts

You've heard it taught that you should not murder and there are lots of ways of killing—like destroying a person's dignity! Whoever does this to his brother is in danger of going straight to hell! So next time you plan to bring an offering to church, think about this; Do something for that man, then give your money! (Based on Matthew 5:21-24.)

AM I A RACIST?

A black man called a group of us racists, God, and I was upset. I've prayed for the Negro, given money to help him, bought a membership in the NAACP, and one of my best friends is black! He really burned me up! But since then I've been thinking; am I a racist, dear God? I never lifted a finger against the black, but I have the haunting feeling I haven't lifted one for him either. I don't discriminate; if one wants to live next door to me, he can! But, I also know we've got some unwritten codes in my neighborhood. He couldn't really buy any house here.

I know I look on the black man as inferior. Even though I've been nice to him I haven't treated him the same as everyone else. Help me to get to know him better so I'll overcome this superiority which is in all us whites.

Then I'll have to admit my religion has been concerned with heaven, souls, the Word, prayers, and little action at the black man's side. I don't want to be a racist, Lord. I want to be a person who lives so others can be persons. Open my mouth so I'll speak up; strengthen my will so I'll live my convictions; stretch my hand so I'll confront the institutions that push all of us into racism.

ENTERTAINMENT

It's the vivid realities surrounding us that mold our thinking and shape our emotions. The cinematic invasion of our living rooms concerns a great many people. Often, parents are all too indifferent to the effect of the tube on their young children's moral computers which are being programmed daily with subtle instructions on white racism, violence, and anti-human emotions. One night when I could stand television no more I wrote the following:

Go watch TV, you've got nothing to do! Try Channel 8; it may have something new!

Westerns, mysteries, news, or spies? Carbines, pistols, clubs, or knives?

Sorry, there's a change in plan, seems they've killed another man—J.F.K., M.L.K., R.F.K., or who? Irishman, nigger, wop, or Jew?

Go watch TV, get out of my way!

Violence, hatred, fill the day. There's sixty hours of tube-filled search.

Oh, well, it's time to go to church!

God Wants Peacemakers

Oh the happiness of those who really work for peace among all men. These are they who will be called the sons of God! (Based on Matthew 5:9.)

SHOW ME THE WAY TO PEACE

The newspaper has a strange combination of stories, Lord Jesus: the bombing of a city and the burning of draft cards. I confess I can't understand those kids; they're not very patriotic! But then, neither am I; I don't seem to be able to do anything to stop that bombing or to help those kids avoid dying foolishly.

Violence is so much a way of life in our world. Show me how to confront it in the worlds I live in—including my church! We don't really speak up much. Neither do we cast our votes for peacemakers. It seems we always make excuses about wars, declared and undeclared.

Be with the young people who are fed up with our warring ways. Teach us how to join hands with them and bring about true peace. Show me, Lord, the way of peace and give me the guts to walk that way.

THE CHURCH CHOIR

I was in a small inner-city church as the summer guest minister. Less than sixty people were scattered throughout the large sanctuary. The choir and the people communicated a total lack of Christian relationship to the seething, troubled world outside those walls. I jotted down some notes while I waited for the time to preach.

> The little choir raised its voice in song.* They weren't very professional and they looked holy enough; but something was wrong.
> "I have a song that Jesus gave me, 'Tis a melody of love," they sang.
> But, my mind was full of discord—like the discord between blacks and whites. That's it, I thought, music consists of black and white notes!
> "I love the Christ who died on Calvary, he washed my sins away."
> But had they really thought? He was a Jew! He was like those isolated in the ghetto or incinerated in an oven! He was isolated from them by design! Our prejudice—our sin—was ever with us!
> "T'will be my endless theme in glory, When the courts of heaven ring."
> We all talk about law and order. We say the courts of earth have been too easy. But, where, O God, has true justice gone? Has it lifted the poor? Has it healed the oppressed? Has it flowed like a mighty stream through our land?
> Then I knew—the theme of glory is the humanization of man. That's my song of praise; with that the angels of heaven join in the chorus.

* From "In My Heart There Rings a Melody," copyright, 1924. Renewal, 1951, by E. M. Roth. Assigned to Hope Publishing Company.

Master Does Strange Thing

It was just before the Jewish holiday celebration of the Passover that Jesus was sitting in a little apartment with his buddies. Mary had invited them there to supper; but Judas was out somewhere else trying to make a deal to get rid of Jesus. In the middle of the meal, Jesus went into the kitchen and came back with a basin of water and soap. He began to wash the dirty feet of the disciples. However, Peter protested, "Look, Jesus, you're supposed to be a big guy doing big things; let's cut out this stuff!" And Jesus said, "There's a reason for this. You'll understand someday." Then Peter said, "Well, you're not washing my feet!" And the Lord answered him, "If I don't, then you can't be my disciple." He was trying to teach Peter that in order to give, you have to know how to receive. He was trying to demonstrate to the disciples that true leadership is based on humble servanthood. (Based on John 13:1-11.)

THE SMALL GROUP IN THE HOME

LEADER: Lord Jesus, just as you gathered with your disciples in that little apartment so many years ago, we know you are here with us as we sit here, close together, in your name. We don't really understand how you can be here and still be with those people in Germany, or Scotland, or Africa, or Russia, but we believe.

OTHERS: Lord, this is our prayer.

LEADER: As you washed the feet of Peter, not only to clean the dirt from sandaled feet, but to show him that cleansing comes from quiet submission to your touch, so clean us.

OTHERS: Lord, this is our prayer.

LEADER: As that same apartment was visited by you after your death, showing how walls cannot keep you out; so be in our thoughts, words, studies, prayers, that we may also find ways to penetrate the walls which life continues to build up.

OTHERS: Lord, this is our prayer.

LEADER: As you led the humble fishermen out of that house into other homes, other segments of society, other towns and cities, confronting them with your will and plan as God gave it to you; send us, O Jesus, with the confidence of victory.

OTHERS: Lord, this is our prayer. Amen.

Minister Prays for Church

"Father," prayed Jesus, "I pray for the church. May they be filled with your joy. I gave them a message to share with the world; help them to pay any price to get that message out. I don't ask you to keep them from harm, anymore than I ask it for myself, but I pray they'll be faithful in the world. As you sent me, so I am sending them." (Based on John 17: 12-18.)

FOR THE LOCAL CHURCH

The minister's getting it in the neck again, Lord Jesus! There's a group in the church that is criticizing him for not visiting enough in the homes. Poor guy! He spends longer hours than they do counseling, visiting hospitals, turning church wheels, and trying to bring up a family, to say nothing of his responsibilities in the community and state. My Lord, how can he stand it? Do something to that church so the man can really be a prophet and priest! Begin in me!

Is there any future for the church, Jesus? A lot of people are asking this. There are times when I have my doubts; then I remember the sacrifice and work that's gone into it. Somehow, I feel you are still counting on those outposts to do the job you intended. Light a fire under it! Stir the members so that the church will begin to count for something. Begin in me. Give me a small number who feel the way I do and push us to action, O Christ, today!

MAN IN THE ROBE

Every Sunday the churchgoer enters that pew and submits to the literary efforts of the man in the robe. My work permits me to frequent a pew more than most clergymen, so I have opportunities to feel and think like a layman.

I once knew a minister who went to his church each Saturday and sat by himself in the empty pews. He spent time prayerfully thinking of those who frequented them. This became my own practice when I was a pastor of a church. Perhaps more ministers and priests should do this and hear what that man in the pew is thinking!

> Man in the robe, do you know I'm here in this pew? You act so tired and weighted by the burdens of growling people and the bleeding world.
>
> Your voice drones on and on and on.
>
> How can I get you to hear me? I'm lost in the jungle of hymnbooks, communion cups, kneeling benches, and offering plates.
>
> Man in the robe, with the same black tie, push-button precision, perfumed holiness, and organ sweetness—can't you hear me?
>
> I'm hoping; I'm waiting; I'm looking; I'm wanting! Show me the love of Jesus—just once!
>
> Drop the jargon! Climb the cross!
>
> Remember? They stripped him of his robe; they gambled by his feet; they spit on him and cursed him; then they killed him. But in his pain he became me.

71

New Leaders Chosen

After this the Lord chose seventy-two key men and brought them together for a training session. "You've got a big job ahead," he said, "and not much help to carry it out. Join with me in praying for more workers, and remember, you're facing a rough road ahead. Remember that you're not interested in power, or money, or things, but you're going out to touch the lives of people. You're going out to change their lives, their homes, and their communities." (Based on Luke 10:1-12.)

REMEMBER THE EXECUTIVES

Father of everybody, we're offering a special prayer on behalf of the executives of our churches. We look up to them as our leaders, believing that you have given them great responsibilities. But keep that from going to their heads; keep them humble and human at all times.

In the midst of the pressures, while they are overwhelmed with decisions and administrative work, may you sit with them at their desks, and ride with them to their appointments. Sensitize them so they'll be more like Jesus and less like the Pharisees.

Big Party Given

Jesus told a story about a man who threw a big party. Invitations had been sent to key people, but when their answers came back, they all had excuses. One had just bought some property he had to check; another had a new car he wanted to try out; another had just married and wasn't about to leave his bride so soon. So the man throwing the party said, "OK, I'll go down into the ghetto and invite the poor, the long-haired, the drunks, and the sickly." A great time was had by all those who came to the big party. (Based on Luke 14:15-24.)

BE WITH THE ECUMENICAL MOVEMENT

God of every church and synagogue, bring oneness to the world through the church. We admit it has been guilty of dividing people; but we also sense that is over. In the spirit of Pope John, and with the steadiness of Martin Luther King, keep us from doing anything that will weaken your people and your world.

Heal the divisions; give us understanding. Bind us in concern; unite us in work, so that our prayers may be one and our actions might be real. Bring peace to your world because the church has learned how to be the model of peace and the channel of love.

Unique Sales Technique Demonstrated

Jesus lectured at a shopping center, and crowds pushed their way to hear him. He saw two counters which salesmen had left unattended. He went behind one counter and began talking to the people.

One of the salesmen, named Pete, came back and Jesus said, "Watch how I do this. I'll sell everything on this counter." Pete said, "I don't believe it. This stuff hasn't been moving." Suddenly the crowd bought everything there and Pete was flabbergasted! He said to Jesus, "You really have something special. You're a better man than I am!" His fellow workers, Jim and Jack, also couldn't believe what they saw. "There's nothing to it," said Jesus. "Just watch me and from now on you'll be really selling in a way you never have before!" They closed up shop, right then, and went with him. (Based on Luke 5:1-11.)

BLESS THE DENOMINATIONAL LEADERS

When we pray for the church, Jesus, we think of those leaders of our denominations and councils who work out of national headquarters. They seem so far away and so removed from us, it's almost frightening. Increase our trust in them, please. Give us new understanding of their jobs. Let them know we're around; that we're the reason they're in business.

We realize that these people have a hard time pleasing everyone. Give them courage to stand up for what is right; give them sweetness of temperament as they try to lead the church from the top. Speak to them frequently so they'll remember why the church is around. Open their eyes to the poor, lonely, and forgotten people of the world. May they be faithful to you and to the promise they made to you so long ago.

7
It's a Special Time
In My Life

Life is made up of special events. There is a rhythm of existence which manifests itself around seasons and events, and the beginning and even ending of eras. So when you live fully this rhythmic pattern, keeping in tune with the major and minor chords, you also develop a prayer style which enables you to celebrate to the fullest. The reason the artist Corita Kent has made such an impact is because she has that capacity to lift up life as a celebration of the presence of God, especially during those special occasions which come to us all.

This has been the most difficult section for me to write because there is something terribly artificial about setting down prayers for certain seasons of the year. Instead, what is shared here actually came out of the events of my life. When a grandchild was born to us I wrote a prayer. I went through the Lenten Season too overwhelmed to write until I returned from church on Palm Sunday morning and wrote "Palm Sunday Tomorrow." The prayer "On a National Holiday" was written on the Fourth of July amidst the popping of firecrackers!

Try writing your own prayers when some special occasion inspires you to put down thoughts and shape phrases which will have meaning for you through many years and may even help another person.

MY CELEBRATION

There's a tragic theme which runs through the Christian ethic of the past; it lifts high the rural life as though it were most godly and downgrades the city as though it were Satan's sole habitat. But times are changing and there is a joyful awareness of the good things associated with urbanization.

One day when my heart was overflowing I sat on a bench in busy Boston Common, among the crowds of people, and the pulse of city movement, and wrote of my feelings.

> Some people feel sorry for me because I live in the city. The sloping mountains, the swaying trees, the rolling hills, and the rushing streams are all in pictures for folks like me.
>
> Each day I shout from the housetops or sing on my way to work because I live in the city and have so much to see.
>
> My trees are straight poles holding wires which connect homes with homes and sadness with joy.
>
> My mountains are high buildings which give bread and heat and light. They please my eye with their shapes and designs.
>
> My grass is the sidewalk with shades and colors no lawns possess; and its lengths stretch endlessly.
>
> My streams are the people rushing to and fro; shuffling, bouncing, dancing to the beat of urban life.
>
> Don't feel sorry for me. I'm celebrating the movements of life. The rush of crowds, the smell of smoke, the noise of traffic, and the sound of voices are all in the City of God.

Jesus Prays for His Own

Father, now I pray for those I love. I don't pray for the others right now; just for those who are extra special because they've decided to follow my way. Since we are one, may your glory shine through me into them. They're facing a cruel world, O holy Father. Keep them safe and beautiful; help them to be one as you and I are one. (Based on John 17:9-11.)

AT THE TIME OF MARRIAGE

Our wedding time is close, O Lord, and I can hardly believe it. This is the happiest moment of my life. Be in that moment, please!

We're both so exhausted from preparations, plans, rehearsals, and celebrations. Keep us from being so tired and numb that we'll miss the real meaning of the day. Keep us fresh, rested, and sensitive to what it's all about.

We know there are a lot of adjustments and a lot of growing up ahead of us, but we love each other enough and believe in your helping us so that we will grow together. May the home we form be full of your peace and your joy, O Jesus. May it always help others to know you're around and a part of our life.

CHRISTMAS HAS COME

Maybe Christmas is overcommercialized but even the decorations outside the stores help to offset the drabness of winter.

I love to walk in the shopping centers and see the gay colors. I love to watch the eager faces of excited little children. I'm also painfully aware of the multitudes of the poor who do not share those joyful experiences. That's why Christmas has meaning for me! It reminds me of the fact that the reason Jesus came was to tell the good news and fill the heart with joy and peace.

> The cold wind slithers across dead grass, muddy land, and snowy piles. Bowed shoulders push against the icy blasts. Life goes on—dull, hard, routine, and tight.
>
> Then comes the night. The lights turn on; the colors shine. The ugly and dreary all light up with Christmas joy.
>
> The burdened are lifted. The dark becomes light. The common is transformed. Drab life has new meaning. Joy to the world! The Lord has come as a bulb in the darkness!

Baby Born in Garage

When the poor people arrived at the garage behind the motel, they found Mary and Joseph there and the new little baby. They were told some strange things about this baby and were excited at what they heard. (Based on Luke 2:16-18.)

ON THE BIRTH OF A CHILD

What a beautiful bit of good news I have received, Lord Jesus; a new baby has arrived and my heart is filled with joy! Bless the parents in their time of great happiness. How marvelous it is that the miracle of their love could result in the creation of a new person. How we thank you for this gift so awesome and striking.

May the thrill these new parents experience never die; may it grow into mature and wholesome love. Give them limitless patience and tender sensitivity so that when the screaming, temper tantrums, lack of obedience, and human mistakes come, these matters will be handled just as you handle their problems. May they always see their role as models and guides but never as neurotics possessively destroying. Help them always to distinguish between abnormal love which so often motivates parents and selfless love which insists a child be himself. As this little one begins to crawl, walk, goo, talk, distinguish, and hear, may all of us be perceived as persons who are like you, O Jesus, sharing wisdom and love which brings peace and goodwill to all people.

Dying Man Speaks to Mother

Standing at the foot of the cross of Jesus were his mother, Mary, wife of Clopas, and Mary Magdalene. Jesus saw his mother with his friend John at her side. He said, "Mom, let John be your son now." And then he said to John, "Friend, she's your mother now." And from then on John had Mary living with him. (Based on John 19:25-27.)

FOR MY MOTHER

O Father, who has the mother-heart concern, hear my prayer. Today I want to remember my mother in this time of prayer. I want to thank you for her and at the same time lift her up in love. I'm sure she thinks that we kids never give a thought of her except on Mother's Day. It's true, we don't show our love as often as we should but I do want to; show me how. Give me a sensitivity to her feelings; patience with her faults; understanding of her needs. When I get too busy to do little thoughtful things for her, kind of remind me with a little whisper from above. Be with me today as I do that little extra thing. May she walk closer to you because I've cared. May those who are around her find ways of bringing happiness to her and may we all continue to receive from her the gifts she has to offer.

Jesus Claims Father's Love

"The Father loves me," said Jesus, "because I'm willing to give up my life in order that I may receive it back again. No one takes my life away from me. I give it up of my own free will. I have the right to give it and I have the right to take it back. That is what the Father has told me to do."

The people around him disagreed over what he meant by this. Some said, "He's nuts! He's positively possessed! Why do people listen to the guy?" Others said, "He's not crazy! A crazy man couldn't say what he's saying or do what he's doing!" (Based on John 10: 17-21.)

FOR MY FATHER

O God, you've tried so often to tell us you are our Father, but we understand this best when we pray for the father you gave us here on earth. Oh sure, he isn't holy, or perfect, or even all-loving; but he is the one who made us possible and he's the one who kept us through hard work and constant love. So bless him in a special way, Lord. May I have new understanding for Dad. Let me see beyond his weak points to the good things that he's contributed to my life. Give him good health, steady heart, and happy days ahead.

STOP ME, IT'S SPRING

Have you ever been so busy that you didn't notice the coming of spring? I have. And suddenly something stopped me and touched my ears, eyes, and nose and this made my heart palpitate. I'd been blind to the miracle about me. It's like sleeping through a circus. I'm glad I woke up in time to enjoy it!

It dropped over my street when I was the busiest. The canopy of spring fell like a carpet with fragrant smell. It was topped by azure skies daubed with kites. It was filled with gnarled trees boasting mantillas and washed houses dressed up with jonquils. Nosy robins playfully probed damp yards amidst bouncing balls, running feet, babbling neighbors, and echoing street.

Stop me; it's spring! Reset my antenna; refocus my camera; retune my smeller, and rewind my music box!

Don't let me run through the miracle of spring.

King Enters City

Jesus headed for the city of Jerusalem. As he approached a suburban area outside the city, he sent two of his followers ahead with instructions: "In the next town you will see a new car parked in front of the little white house on the corner of Main and Spruce. Here's the key. Bring it to me. If someone from the house is there, tell them the Master needs it. They'll understand. That's why they gave me the key." So they took the car to Jesus. As he rode slowly along the road, people went in front of him and gave great cheers! "Look," they cried out, "here he is, the King who comes in the name of the Lord! He comes to bring peace and to give glory to God!"

Some of the religious leaders spoke up from the crowd and shouted to Jesus saying, "Tell them to shut up!" And Jesus shouted back, "If they do shut up, even the pavement on this street will begin to shout!" (Based on Matthew 21:1-11.)

HOLY WEEK IS HERE

Dear Jesus:

Holy Week has rolled around again. It kind of brings me to a halt as I think of what happened in your life.

Funny, so much will be happening in churches this week. I wonder if it makes you sick? All the words, I mean. So much noise is made and still we haven't dug up the cross yet!

Then next week it will all be a memory. O Christ, how long can this go on? Shake the clergy loose from their imprisonment in ritual! Make me, as a guy who thinks about these things, face up to this whole bag of dying and living for you! Amen.

84

PALM SUNDAY TOMORROW

Palm Sunday is always one of the most difficult days of the Christian year for me. There is so much made of the historical event so familiar to all. Sometimes one gets the feeling that it has its place among situations of the past like "George Washington slept here," or "This is where John F. Kennedy delivered his famous speech." But the Palm Sunday invasion of Jesus is more than that. It is a contemporary experience; always happening and always touching the lives of all people.

> Jesus entered Tokyo on scarred bike 'mid rebel thrust and campus dust; 'mid rocks, mace, clubs, and throngs. He stood with chanting students and swinging clubs. He heard the political slogans shouted; he felt the crush of youth; he listened to the wailing minor chords and wrote his song.
>
> Jesus entered Mexico on an overflowing bus 'mid festive crowds. He watched the rockets shoot skyward, smelled the flowers, tasted the tacos, and danced to the mariachis. He thrilled to the rhythm and shouts of laughter. The music blended with the joy which drowned out care.
>
> Jesus entered Washington on rumbling tank 'mid roaring flames and rebel guns. He received cries, curses, screams, and heat. The rotunda echoed with marching feet; the black revolutionary bound up wounds on the blood-soaked street.
>
> Jesus entered Circleville in Oldsmobile 'mid blooming buds and Easter scent. He was engulfed by the sanitized, white, peaceful pall. The lilting hymns, frosty prayers, pretty sermons, and waving palms made him sick. He's the itinerant carpenter but the houses are all built!

EASTER'S COME AGAIN

When will the Christian really learn that Easter happens more than one day a year? When will the mature believer grasp the fact that the profound good news of the presence of the living, risen Christ is what really makes the difference?

As a pastor, I confess there were always doubts about the things I preached on Easter. I honestly thought I was mouthing some truths to make people feel better, until I sat at a bedside and watched a man die; or until I joined in prayer with a mother who had just lost her little boy. Then I felt His presence; I knew He was at our side. The gripping belief of the centuries overwhelmed me; I knew the story was true! Life had new meaning!

> I've been through a lot of them. Warm Sundays; cold Sundays; sunrise services; sunrise breakfasts; hilltop crowds; jammed sanctuaries; trumpet sounds; lily smells; and I still tremble before the mystery of death. I hear the promise of life, resurrection, and hope; but my heart wonders.
>
> Still the man looks awfully dead; still the widow sobs through lonely hours. The doubts rise in my breast; am I kidding myself? Is there more? Will we live forever?
>
> I sit by the hospital bed; the thin hand holds mine; the last gasps of breath come harder; eyes open to meet mine; lips move; she whispers the cry of the ages: "I believe." No organs; no new clothes; no hymns; no angels; no sermons; but the smile of life.
>
> I can't explain it; I can't argue it; I can't prove it; but He **is** there; she sees Him and I see Him too!

Dead Man Found Alive!

It was reported in the Jerusalem news that two men were riding a bus from Jerusalem to the suburb of Emmaus. They were deeply engrossed in discussing the assassination of Jesus, the troublemaker, when a man sat next to them. He joined in the conversation and they told him that they were disappointed in losing such a great leader! They also shared the rumor that his body had disappeared from the grave and that some hysterical women even said he was really alive!

According to the two men, the stranger then began to talk to them about the Bible and how it predicted such things would happen. They were so intrigued that when they came to their stop, they invited him to join them for dinner. He did. But during the meal they suddenly saw that this man appeared to be Jesus! And then, they later reported, he was gone! They were convinced it was Jesus! They also said he had ignited fire within them that never would go out! They called the newspaper and shouted over the phone, "Christ is alive; they couldn't destroy him!" (Based on Luke 24:13-35.)

IT'S EASTER EVERY DAY!

Man alive! That's great news! Jesus lives, speaks, and loves! He is here among us! That's what it means, God! No casket can hold him, no police state can hold him back, no church can keep him to themselves, no politicians can vote him away, no noise can drown his voice, and no hate can limit his love. That's beautiful; thank you, God, for Easter!

Lepers Healed Miraculously

As Jesus drove to Jerusalem, He took the cutoff road between Samaria and Galilee. He saw ten lepers by the road. They all yelled, "Jesus! Master! Help us, please!" He stopped the car and said, "I'll take you to the clinic. Hop in." They went with him to the clinic. As they got out of the car, they saw their leprosy had disappeared. They went running to tell the doctors at the clinic what had happened. But one of the lepers came back to Jesus and said, "Thank you." Jesus said to him, "There were ten healed, where are the other nine?" Then he added, "Get up and go; your faith has made you well." (Based on Luke 17: 11-19.)

IT'S THANKSGIVING

Jesus, it's Thanksgiving time; and turkeys, football games, and family gatherings are here again. Funny, how seldom we think of giving thanks except on that one day. Thank you over and over again for everything I have and everyone I know. Thank you, Jesus, for life and all it has meant to me. Thank you for my friends, family, and loved ones. Thank you for my car, my home, my job, and the little things I take for granted. And, Lord, show me how I can really express my gratitude to those around me.

Youth Sees Christ Alive!

One of Jesus' disciples was not around when he first appeared to the others. He was young Tom, the twin. The others enthusiastically reported, "We saw Jesus alive!" Tom said, "Come on, I don't believe it; in fact I wouldn't believe it unless I saw the nail prints in his hands and touched them, and the hole in his side!"

A week later the disciples and Tom were having a bite to eat at Tom's house when, even though the doors were locked, Jesus stood right in front of them. "Peace be with you," he said to the scared men. Then he said to Tom, "So you don't believe I'm alive? OK, put your fingers here on my hands and check out the scar in my side." Tom fell to his knees and said, "My Lord—my God!" Then Jesus said, "You've now believed because you've seen with your own eyes, but the real believer is the one who doesn't have to have outward proof like you do!" (Based on John 20:24-29.)

AT GRADUATION TIME

We're about to march down the aisle to the familiar graduation tune of "Pomp and Circumstance." Man, it's been a long road, it seems, to this time. Thank you for being with me, Lord, through studies and all the rest.

I'm a little scared to think what's ahead. It just came to me that this is it! I'm going out into the world and I'm not sure I'm prepared. Be by my side; carry me over the rough spots. As I make the next decisions in life and turn in new directions, hold me up with your wise thinking and your endless loving.

Loyalty to Country Urged

Some of the opposition were sent to trick Jesus with some questions. They said, "We know you'll play square with us. Tell us, man, what do you think of all these taxes? Should we pay them?" But Jesus saw what they were driving at, so he said, "Hold out a coin; whose picture's on it?" They answered, "The president's." So Jesus said, "Well, pay to him what's owed and give to God what's owed him." And they were surprised at how brilliant he was. (Based on Mark 12: 13-17.)

ON A NATIONAL HOLIDAY

The flags are waving; the bands are playing; but most people have forgotten what this day is all about, Lord. They're picnicking, boating, and eating while the real meaning of the holiday has been lost. Patriotism is hard to find; maybe it's because we thought of it in such limited terms—like flag-waving, gun-carrying, and speeches. Let us see all over again what it really means.

Make us recover the spirit of the patriots when people were most important and freedom was a way of life. Lift our love for country so it's not blind, ignoring the weaknesses and faults which grip us. Lead us as a nation to that level where we can see ourselves critically and still act unselfishly. Eliminate the image of the ugly American and put in its place the true patriot who gives his life to bring out the best within us. Unite us with a sense of brotherhood which achieves justice for all and peace forever.

Index of Poems

Index of Prayers

Index of Sidewalk Versions Based upon Scriptures

Index of Subjects